posh®

A-**MAZE**-ING
PLACES

Andrews McMeel Publishing
a division of Andrews McMeel Universal
1130 Walnut Street, Kansas City, Missouri 64106

www.andrewsmcmeel.com

A-MAZE-ING PLACES first published in 2017 by Hinkler Books Pty Ltd.
45-55 Fairchild Street
Heatherton Victoria 3202 Australia
© 2017 by Susanna Geoghegan Gift Publishing

18 19 20 21 22 RLP 10 9 8 7 6 5 4 3 2 1

ISBN: 978-1-4494-9510-7

Library of Congress Control Number: 2018930597
Editor: Jean Z. Lucas
Art Director: Julie Barnes
Production Editor: Maureen Sullivan
Production Manager: Tamara Haus

ATTENTION: SCHOOLS AND BUSINESSES
Andrews McMeel books are available at quantity discounts with
bulk purchase for educational, business, or sales promotional use.
For information, please e-mail the Andrews McMeel Publishing
Special Sales Department: specialsales@amuniversal.com.

posh®

A-MAZE-ING PLACES

Challenging Mazes for the Daydreaming Traveler

Andrews McMeel
PUBLISHING®

MACHU PICCHU

* The ancient city of Machu Picchu was built high in the Andes Mountains in Peru without using any iron tools or wheels.

* The site consists of 170 buildings and over 600 terraces to prevent flooding or slippage of the buildings.

* The most popular way to reach the site is to walk the Inca Trail, which is nearly 26 miles long and reaches heights of up to 13,825 feet above sea level.

MODERATE

MECCA

* Mecca is the most holy city of Islam and the birthplace of the Prophet Mohammed.

* Only Muslims are allowed to enter Mecca, and its Great Mosque can hold up to 1 million worshippers at a time.

* The focal point of Mecca is a cube-shaped building called the Ka'bah ("House of God"), which is covered for most of the year with a gold-embroidered black cloth.

BIG BEN

* Big Ben is actually the name of the giant bell inside the tower at the Palace of Westminster.

* The tower was called the Clock Tower until 2012, when it was renamed Elizabeth Tower in honor of the Queen's Diamond Jubilee.

* The clock's four dials are each almost 23 feet across, and the hour hands are 9 feet long.

MODERATE

EIFFEL TOWER

* The Eiffel Tower is 1,063 feet tall (including antennas) and weighs 7,300 tons.

* In cold weather, the tower shrinks by about 6 inches.

* Every seven years the tower is repainted, using 60 tons of paint.

EASY

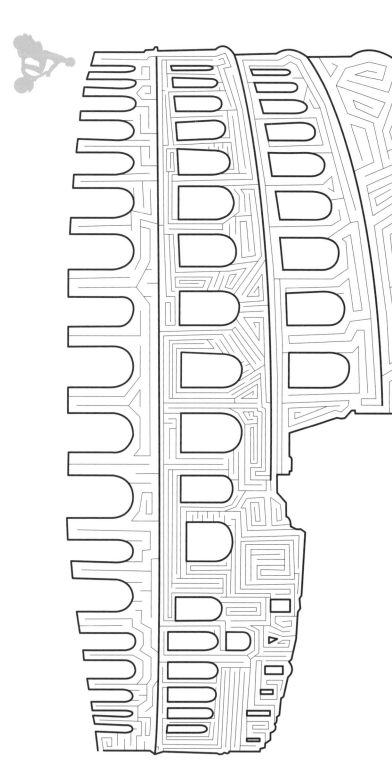

THE COLOSSEUM

* The name "Colosseum" comes from the Latin word "colosseus" meaning "colossal."

* Gladiatorial games held at the Colosseum were performed in front of up to 80,000 Romans.

* Around 4 million visitors to Rome explore the Colosseum each year.

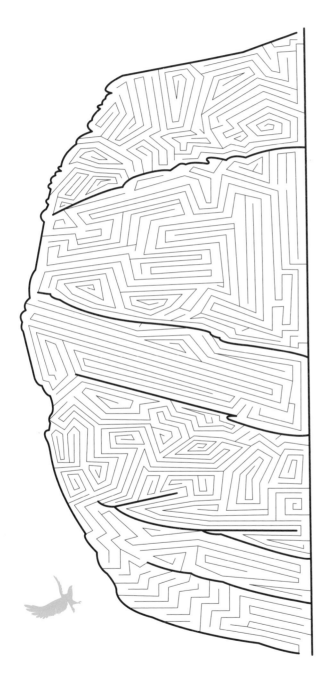

ULURU

* Uluru is the official and Aboriginal name for Ayers Rock, which is located in Australia's Red Centre.

* This huge sandstone monolith was created over 600 million years ago and has a height of 1,142 feet.

* Uluru has a 5.8-mile circumference, and the climb to the top is 1 mile, although its traditional caretakers, the Anangu, do not climb it due to its spiritual significance.

DIFFICULT

THE STATUE OF LIBERTY

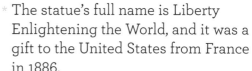

* The statue's full name is Liberty Enlightening the World, and it was a gift to the United States from France in 1886.

* The Statue of Liberty measures 305 feet from the ground to the top of the torch and weighs 225 tons.

* The seven rays on the statue's crown represent the world's seven continents.

EASY

THE BURJ AL ARAB

* The Burj al Arab is a luxury hotel, built at an estimated cost of $1 billion on an artificial island.

* The building's design resembles the billowing sail of a traditional Arab vessel, the dhow.

* A variety of sporting events have taken place on the hotel's helipad, including a friendly tennis match between Roger Federer and Andre Agassi!

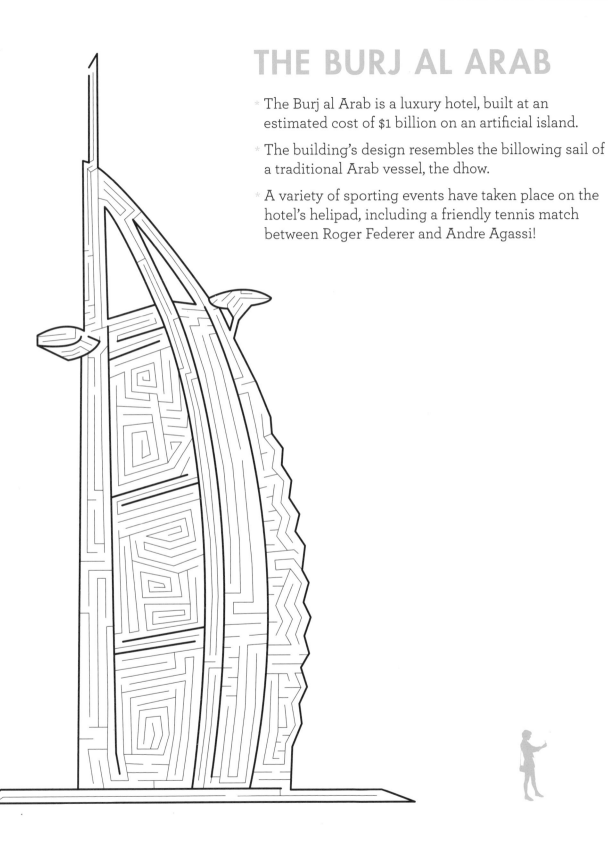

EASY

WINDSOR CASTLE

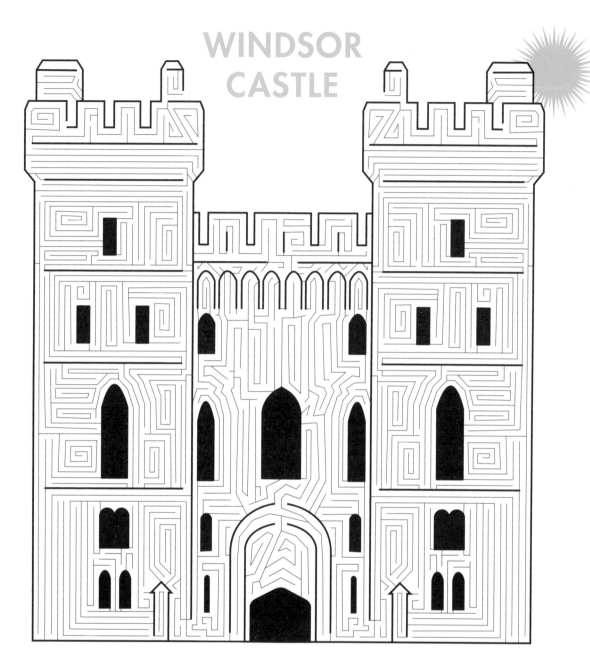

* Windsor Castle is the oldest and largest inhabited castle in the world.

* During World War II, some of the Royal Family secretly slept here instead of at Buckingham Palace. The windows of the castle were blacked out for safety, and the most valuable artworks were moved away.

* In 1992, around 20 percent of the castle was destroyed by fire. The fire took 15 hours to put out, and the restoration cost nearly $4.86 million.

LEANING TOWER OF PISA

* The Leaning Tower of Pisa weighs 15,984 tons.

* The tower took over 200 years to completely finish and began to lean during its construction.

* The tower is 183 feet tall on the lowest side and 186 feet on the highest side.

TAJ MAHAL

* It's estimated that 22,000 people worked on the construction of the Taj Mahal.

* More than 1,000 elephants transported the construction materials used to build it.

* Each of the four sides of the Taj Mahal is perfectly identical.

EASY

PETRONAS TWIN TOWERS

* The Petronas Twin Towers in Kuala Lumpur stand 1,483 feet high from ground level.

* Each tower weighs 330,693 tons (the equivalent of 42,857 elephants!) and has ten escalators.

* The stainless steel and glass design of the towers reflects Islamic geometric patterns.

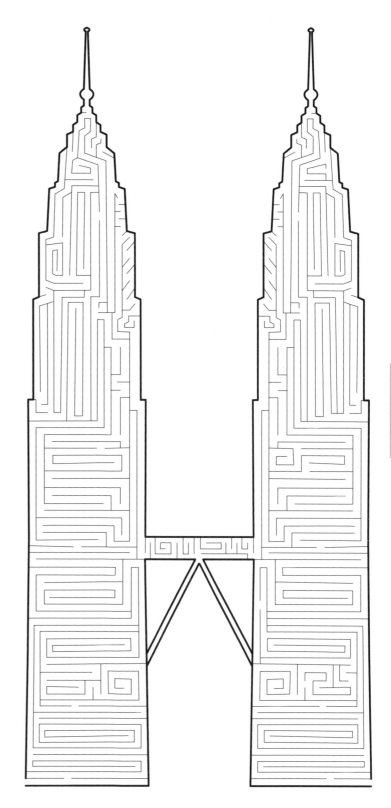

MODERATE

SYDNEY OPERA HOUSE

* Over 7 million people visit the Sydney Opera House every year; about 1.2 million of these attend a performance.

* The opera house was designed by Jorn Utzon, an architect from Denmark.

* The main concert hall can seat almost 2,700 people and contains one of the world's largest organs—it has 10,000 pipes.

DIFFICULT

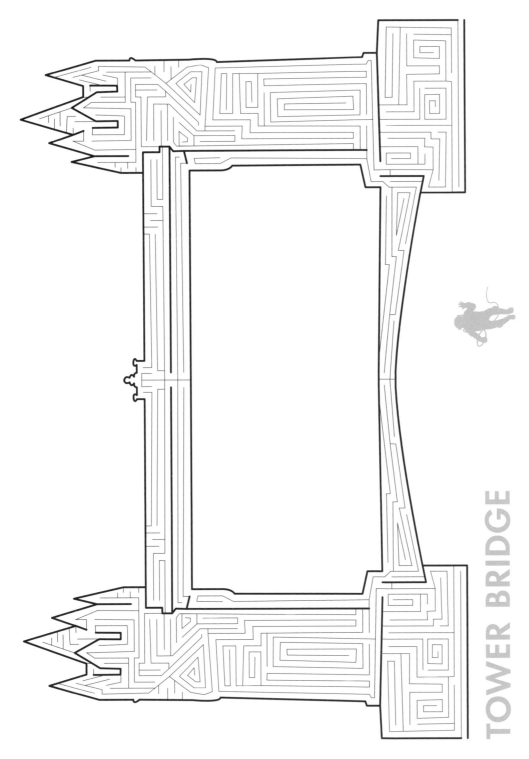

TOWER BRIDGE

* Tower Bridge opened in 1894 after more than 400 workers spent eight years building it.

* The bridge is 801 feet long and has two towers that are 213 feet tall.

* Two movable roadways called bascules lift up for passing ships approximately 777 times a year.

EASTER ISLAND STATUES

MODERATE

* Easter Island is a small volcanic island 2,274 miles off the coast of Chile and is the home of 887 enormous stone statues called "moai."

* Each statue represents the deceased head of a family ancestry line and would take five or six men up to a year to carve using basalt stone chisels.

* The stone heads that are visible aboveground are now being excavated to reveal stone torsos beneath them!

THE LOUVRE

* The Louvre was originally built as a fortress in 1190, and it was only in 1793 that it became a museum.

* It would take around 100 days to look at each item in the Musée du Louvre for 30 seconds.

* The glass Louvre Pyramid is made up of 793 diamond- and triangular-shaped panes of glass.

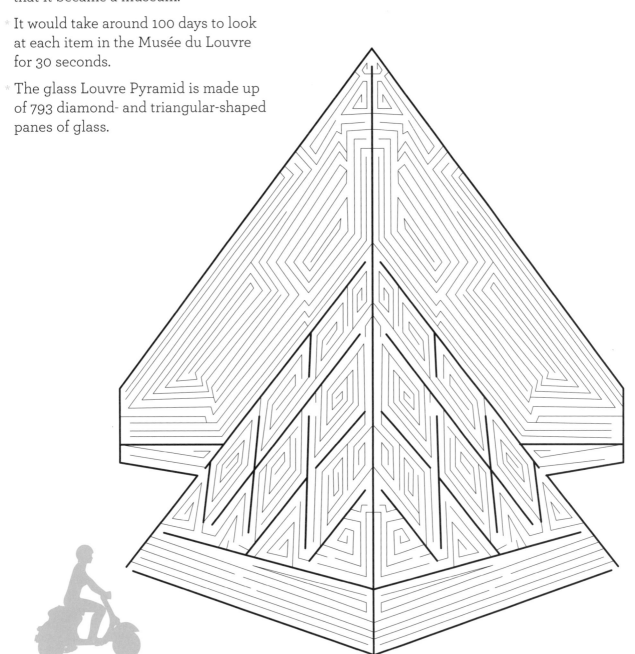

MODERATE

SAGRADA FAMÍLIA

* Construction on the Expiatory Temple of the Holy Family (or Sagrada Família) began in 1882. It is still ongoing and has an estimated completion date of 2026!

* Antoni Gaudí took over as architect in 1883 and eventually gave up nearly all of his other artistic work to focus on the project. He was buried there after his death in 1926.

* Up to 3 million people visit the site every year, making it Barcelona's most visited tourist attraction.

EASY

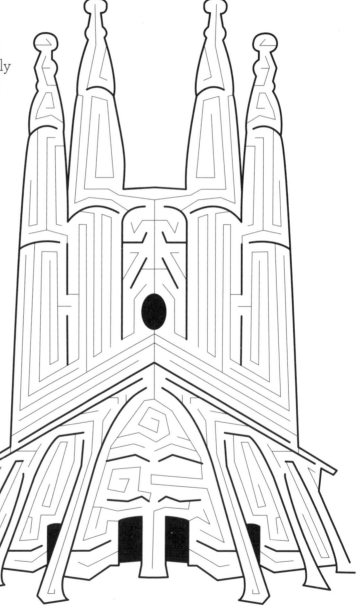

ST. PAUL'S CATHEDRAL

* A cathedral dedicated to St. Paul has existed at the highest point of the city of London since 604 CE, including a version that burned down during the Great Fire of London in 1666.

* Sir Christopher Wren was both the current cathedral's architect and the first person to be buried there.

* The dome at St. Paul's Cathedral is the second largest in the world after St. Peter's in Rome.

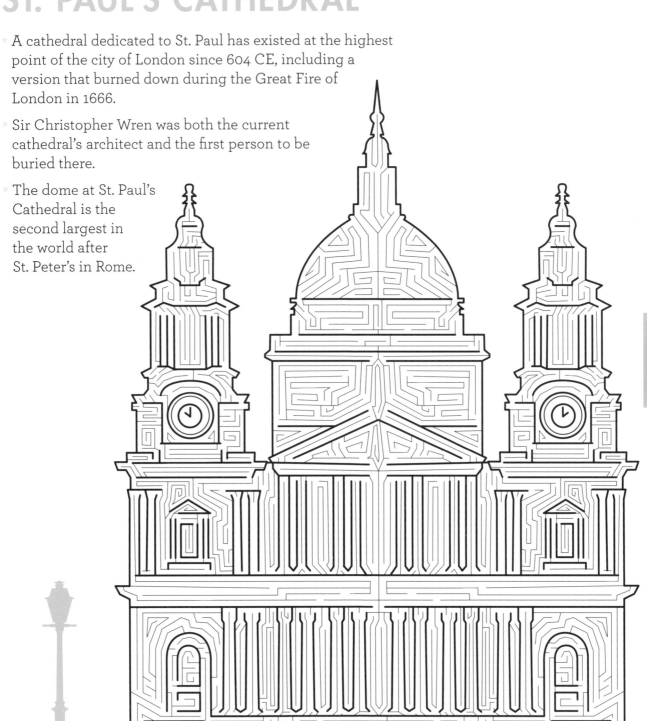

DIFFICULT

THE PENTAGON

* The Pentagon is home to the U.S. Department of Defense and is located in Arlington County, Virginia.

* There are 17.5 miles of hallways over five floors above ground and two basement levels.

* As well as being the largest office building in the world, the Pentagon has six different zip codes.

EASY

TOWER OF LONDON

* The Tower of London was originally built by William the Conqueror and has been used as a prison and a fortress, as well as a royal palace, zoo, and mint.

* Sir Walter Raleigh, Lady Jane Grey, and Anne Boleyn were all imprisoned and subsequently executed at the tower.

* Today, the Tower of London is open to the public as a museum and houses the Crown Jewels.

DIFFICULT

PARLIAMENT HILL

* Parliament Hill, known as "the Hill," sits on the southern banks of the Ottawa River in Ottawa, Ontario.

* The Gothic-style building has hundreds of gargoyles carved into its stone walls.

* Parliament Hill is the political and cultural heart of the city and is where the Canadian parliament meets.

MODERATE

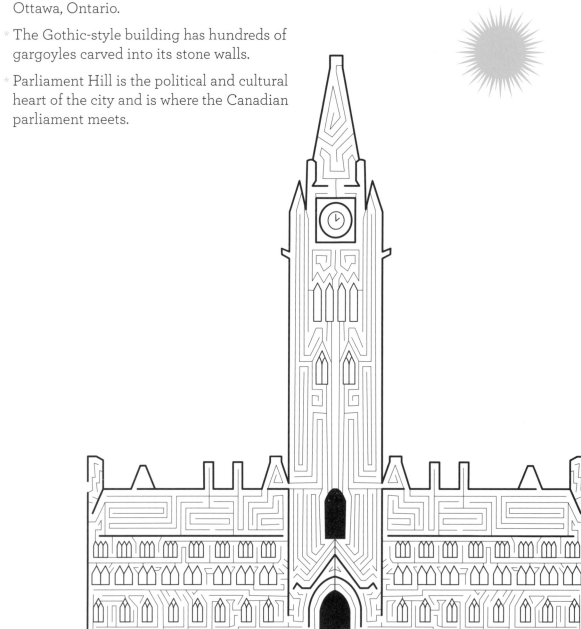

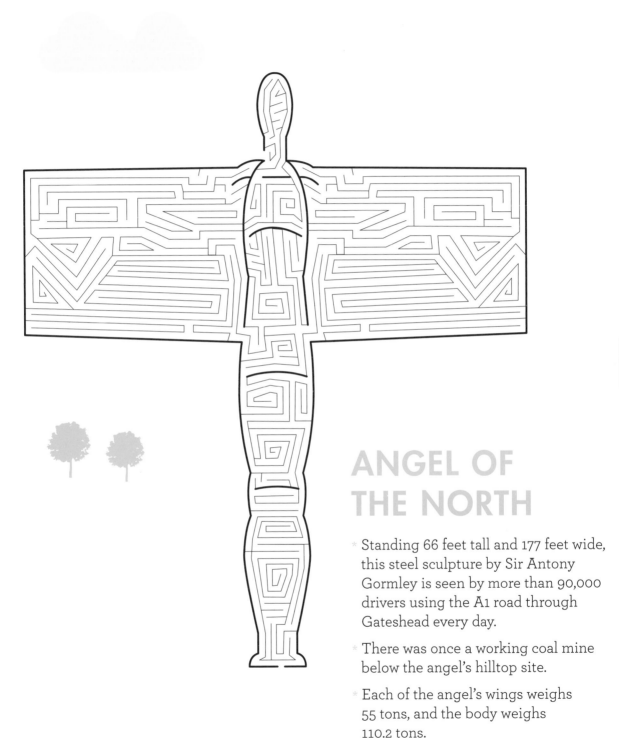

ANGEL OF THE NORTH

* Standing 66 feet tall and 177 feet wide, this steel sculpture by Sir Antony Gormley is seen by more than 90,000 drivers using the A1 road through Gateshead every day.

* There was once a working coal mine below the angel's hilltop site.

* Each of the angel's wings weighs 55 tons, and the body weighs 110.2 tons.

PYRAMIDS OF GIZA

* The three Pyramids of Giza were constructed on the banks of the Nile around 2700–2500 BCE.
* The Great Pyramid of Giza is the only monument remaining of the Seven Wonders of the Ancient World.
* 2.3 million limestone blocks made up the Great Pyramid, creating an original height from base to tip of 480.6 feet.

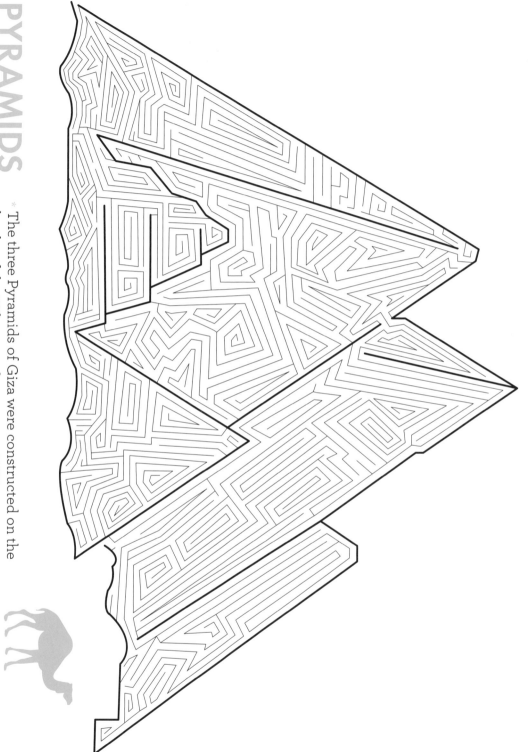

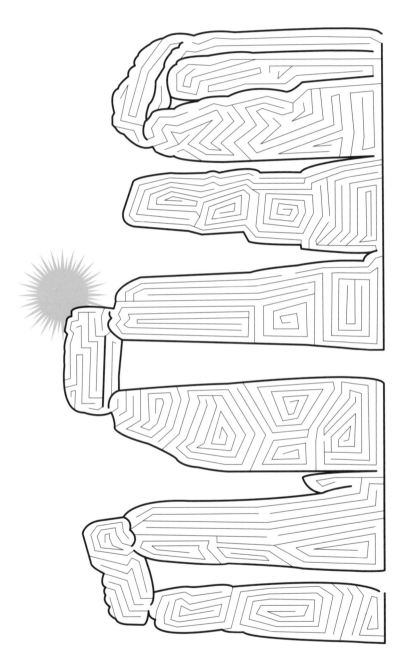

STONEHENGE

* Stonehenge is a circle of standing stones located on Salisbury Plain in Wiltshire.

* It's believed that the stones themselves were erected around 2500 BCE and weigh between 4.4 and 27.5 tons each.

* There are 83 stones at the site, which is the most well known of over 900 stone ring sites in the British Isles.

ARC DE TRIOMPHE

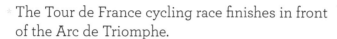

* At 49 feet wide and 95 feet tall, the arch opening was large enough for a biplane to safely fly through it at the end of World War I.

* The Tour de France cycling race finishes in front of the Arc de Triomphe.

* There are 284 steps from ground level to the top of the arc, which is positioned at the center of 12 avenues named after French military leaders.

MODERATE

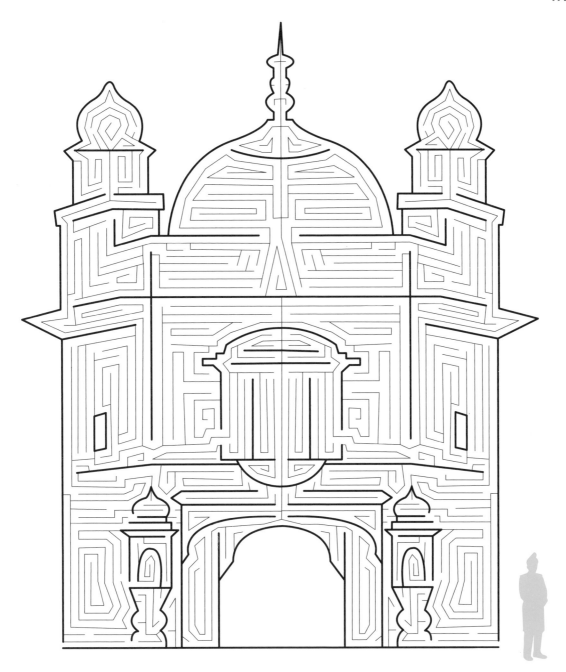

GOLDEN TEMPLE

* The upper part of the Golden Temple was only covered with real gold two centuries after its initial construction in the early sixteenth century.

* The four entrances facing the north, east, south, and west symbolize the Sikh religion's openness to all other people and religions.

* The temple stands in the middle of a man-made pool called "Amrit Sarovar," from which the city of Amritsar gets its name.

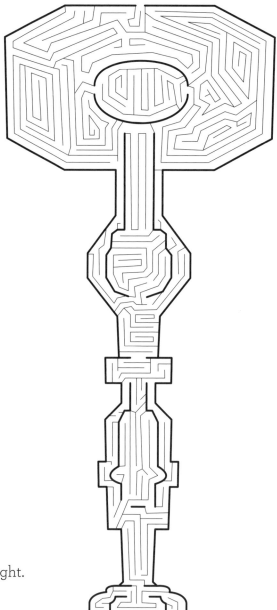

BRIGHTON PIER

* Brighton Palace Pier opened in 1899.
  It cost $36,174 to build—equivalent to
  $2,679,564 today.

* 67,000 lights illuminate the pier every night.

* Visitors to the pier can have fun on the
  fairground rides, visit the shops, and enjoy
  fish and chips or a stick of rock candy.

CN TOWER

* At 1,815.39 feet high, the CN Tower in Toronto is the tallest tower in the Western Hemisphere.

* When the tower was completed in 1976, a time capsule was tucked into its walls. It won't be opened until 2076.

* Once they're attached to a secure harness, visitors can walk around a ledge at the top of the tower.

FLATIRON BUILDING

* The distinctive triangular-shaped Flatiron Building was built in 1902 and sits on the intersection of Fifth Avenue and Broadway.

* At 22 stories high, 307 feet, it's not the tallest building in New York, but it is one of the most unusual—the original elevators were water powered.

* When it was first built, people thought the building would fall because of its shape, but it's constructed around a strong skeleton of steel, covered with limestone and terra-cotta.

MODERATE

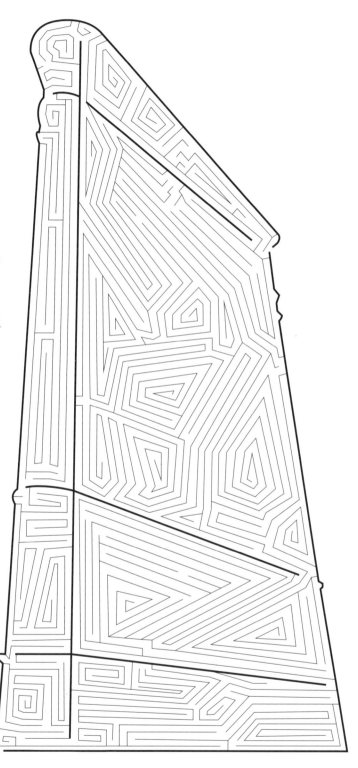

BLUE MOSQUE

* Called Sultanahmet Camii in Turkish, the mosque is known as the Blue Mosque because of the 20,000 blue ceiling tiles inside.

* Sultan Ahmet I commissioned the mosque when he was only 19 years old and was so eager to bring it to life he is believed to have helped build it. He died just a year after its completion at the age of 27.

* Unusually, this mosque has six minarets instead of the usual one, two, or four, which makes it easy to distinguish against the Istanbul skyline.

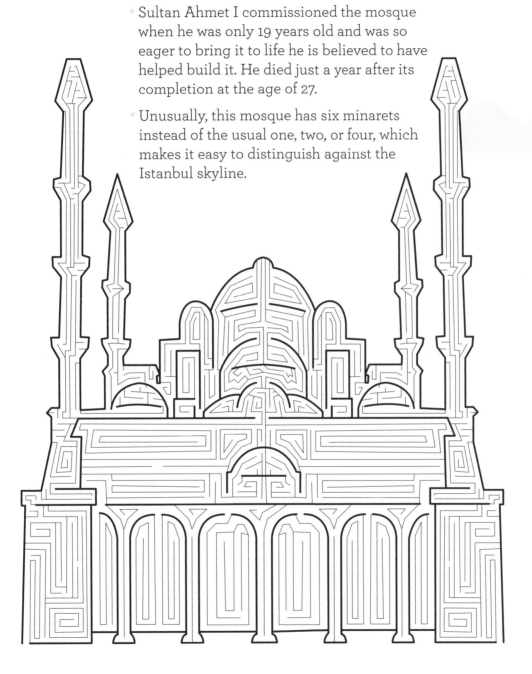

DIFFICULT

HAMPTON COURT PALACE

* In the thirteenth century, long before it became a palace for kings and queens, Hampton Court was a great barn or hall.

* Toward the end of his reign, King Henry VIII spent much of his time at Hampton Court. The ghost of his fifth wife, Catherine Howard, is said to haunt the palace.

* There are 60 acres of gardens, including 8,000 trees and the United Kingdom's oldest hedge maze.

EASY

ST. PETER'S BASILICA

* 551 steps lead from the interior of St. Peter's Basilica to the top of the dome, or cupola, within. Taking the elevator reduces the climb by around 320 steps!

* Designed by Michelangelo and completed after his death, the famous dome is 448 feet high and 138 feet wide.

* A vast underground crypt at the Basilica houses the tombs of many former popes.

THE GREAT SPHINX

* The Great Sphinx statue has the face of the ancient Egyptian ruler, Khafre, who built it, and the body of Ra, the sun god.

* This huge sculpture was carved from an outcropping of limestone left over from the construction of the Great Pyramid of Giza.

* The paws of the Sphinx are 49 feet long, and the face is 13 feet wide.

MOUNT RUSHMORE

* The granite faces carved into Mount Rushmore in the Black Hills region of South Dakota are around 60 feet high, and the project took 14 years to complete.

* From left to right, the four U.S. presidents are George Washington, Thomas Jefferson, Theodore Roosevelt, and Abraham Lincoln.

* Mount Rushmore National Memorial is visited by around 3 million people each year.

DIFFICULT

KENNEDY SPACE CENTER

* The Kennedy Space Center (KSC) is a spaceport, named after President John F. Kennedy.

* Since the 1960s all manned spaceflights have launched from the KSC.

* In 1969 Neil Armstrong and Buzz Aldrin blasted off for the moon from the KSC.

EASY

BATTERSEA POWER STATION

* Built in the early 1930s, Battersea Power Station is the largest brick building in Europe.

* Each chimney is 337 feet tall. The power station provided one-fifth of London's total electricity supplies, and the building was seen as a symbol of the electricity industry.

* The last part of the power station was decommissioned in 1983, and the building has been redeveloped into apartments and shops.

EASY

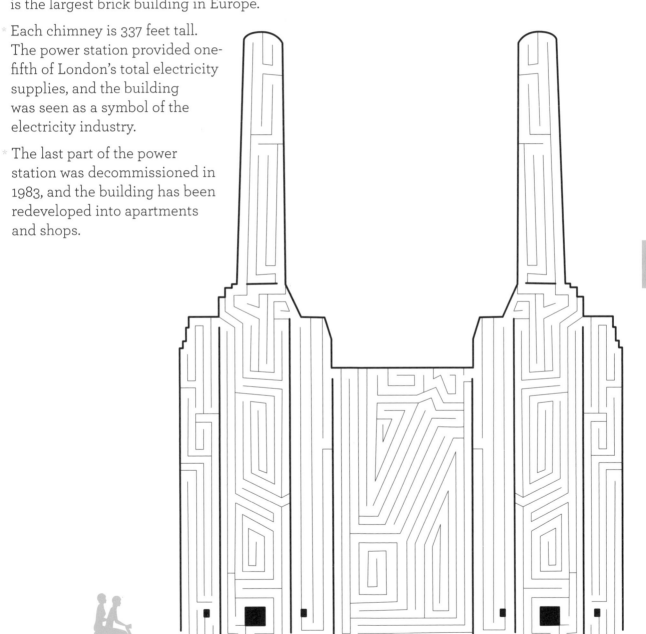

ST. BASIL'S CATHEDRAL

* St. Basil's Cathedral was commissioned in the sixteenth century by Ivan the Terrible to commemorate a military victory.

* The Russian Orthodox cathedral contains nine chapels and a maze of galleries; narrow staircases and low arches connect them from inside.

* Situated in Moscow's Red Square, its official name is the Cathedral of the Intercession of the Blessed Virgin on the Moat.

DIFFICULT

NEUSCHWANSTEIN CASTLE

* The fairytale design of Neuschwanstein Castle inspired the Sleeping Beauty Castle in Disneyland in California.

* The castle was built by King Ludwig II of Bavaria for his sole occupancy. It was due to take three years to build but actually took 17 years, eventually being completed in 1886 after the king's death.

* Neuschwanstein means "new swan stone" and comes from the name of a character in a Wagner opera.

EASY

THE RADCLIFFE CAMERA

* Built between 1737 and 1749, the Radcliffe Camera is a large circular building with a high dome and is part of Oxford University.

* It is the first example of a round library in England. The word "camera" means "room" in Italian.

* Well-known graduates of Oxford University include Oscar Wilde, J.R.R. Tolkien, and Prime Minister Theresa May.

DIFFICULT

PETRA

* A .75-mile walk through a narrow rocky gorge in the Jordanian desert leads visitors into this ancient city of tombs and temples carved from sheer rock faces.

* The most recognizable facade cut into the rose-pink rock deep within Petra is the Treasury, which was carved as a tomb for an important Nabataean king around the first century CE.

* Petra was used as a filming location for the film *Indiana Jones and the Last Crusade* and was named one of the New Seven Wonders of the World in 2007.

MODERATE

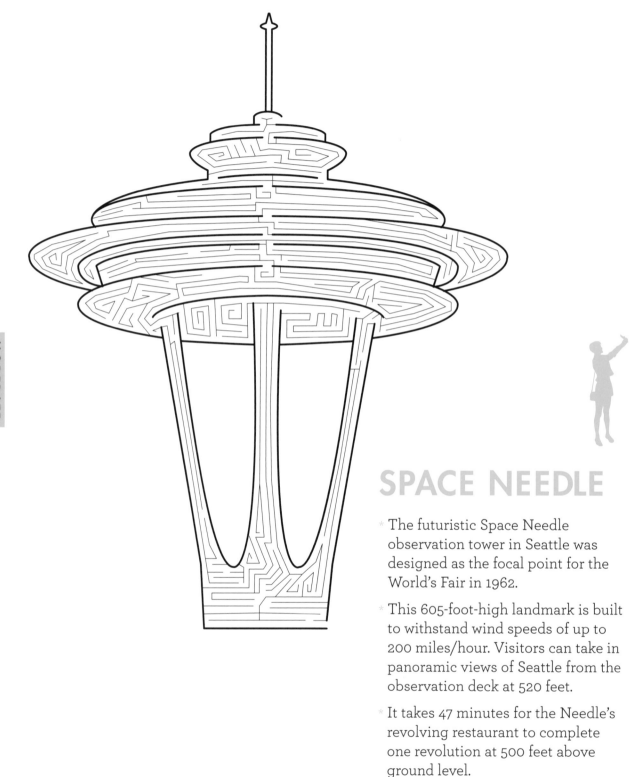

SPACE NEEDLE

* The futuristic Space Needle observation tower in Seattle was designed as the focal point for the World's Fair in 1962.

* This 605-foot-high landmark is built to withstand wind speeds of up to 200 miles/hour. Visitors can take in panoramic views of Seattle from the observation deck at 520 feet.

* It takes 47 minutes for the Needle's revolving restaurant to complete one revolution at 500 feet above ground level.

THE GHERKIN

* Nine red aircraft warning lights glow as darkness falls to alert planes to the height of 30 St. Mary Axe (the Gherkin's official name).

* 7,429 panes of glass and 21.7 miles of steel were used in the construction of the Gherkin, and its elevators travel at speeds of 19.7 feet per second.

* The Gherkin is almost as wide as it is tall. In fact, there's only a 6.6-foot difference between its height and its widest circumference!

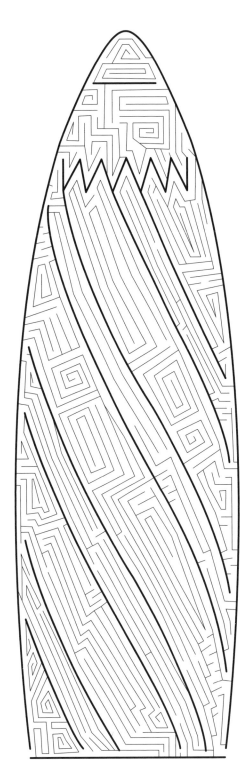

MODERATE

POMPIDOU CENTRE

* The centre is named after Georges Pompidou, who was the president of France from 1969-1974. Pompidou commissioned the building, which opened in 1977.

* Inside the Pompidou Centre is the National Museum of Modern Art, which holds the largest collection of modern art in Europe.

* The building exterior is painted in primary colors, with exposed pipes, escalators, and elevators on the outside of the building.

THE MATTERHORN

* The jagged tooth-like shape of the Matterhorn makes it an Alpine landmark, despite being only the twelfth-highest mountain in Western Europe at 14,692 feet.

* The mountain straddles the border of Switzerland and Italy.

* The Matterhorn was first summited in 1865. However, four of the victorious team of seven climbers died during the descent.

GREAT BUDDHA STATUE

DIFFICULT

* The Great Buddha of Kamakura is the second-largest monumental Buddha in Japan, where giant Buddhas are called "Daibutsu."

* This 44-foot-high Great Buddha sits in the lotus position and weighs 93 tons.

* The bronze statue was cast in 1252 and has been exposed to the elements since the wooden temple that housed it was washed away in a tsunami in 1495.

SACRÉ-COEUR

* The Basilica of the Sacred Heart (Basilique Sacré-Coeur) sits atop the highest point in Paris, in Montmartre.

* The gleaming white material that Sacré-Coeur is built from is a frost-resistant travertine that bleaches with age, called Château-Landon stone.

* The great bell inside Sacré-Coeur, known as the Savoyarde, is one of the heaviest in the world, weighing 19 tons.

MODERATE

ATOMIUM

* Standing 335 feet high, the Atomium's nine steel-clad interconnected spheres combine sculpture with architecture.

* The Atomium was built for the 1958 World's Fair (Expo 58), and its shape is based on an iron crystal, enlarged 165 billion times!

* The spheres house exhibitions and a panoramic restaurant. Visitors can even spend the night there.

EASY

RIALTO BRIDGE

* The Rialto Bridge is the oldest of the four bridges spanning the Grand Canal in Venice.

* Originally built from wood, the Rialto Bridge burned down or collapsed three times before it was constructed from marble in 1591.

* The existing bridge took three years to build after a number of architects and artists—including Michelangelo—submitted designs for it.

EMPIRE STATE BUILDING

* The lightning rod on the Empire State Building is struck by lightning around 23 times per year.

* There are 1,872 steps to the 103rd floor at the top of the building, and each year a race to run from street level to the 86th floor is held. The athletes taking part must climb an exhausting 1,576 steps to victory!

* The antenna at the top of the Empire State Building is used to broadcast most of the commercial TV and FM radio stations in New York City.

EASY

THE PANTHEON

* The Pantheon is one of the best-preserved buildings from Ancient Rome.

* Completed in 125 CE, during the reign of the emperor Hadrian, the Pantheon has been both a temple and a church.

* There are many tombs inside the church, including that of the artist Raphael.

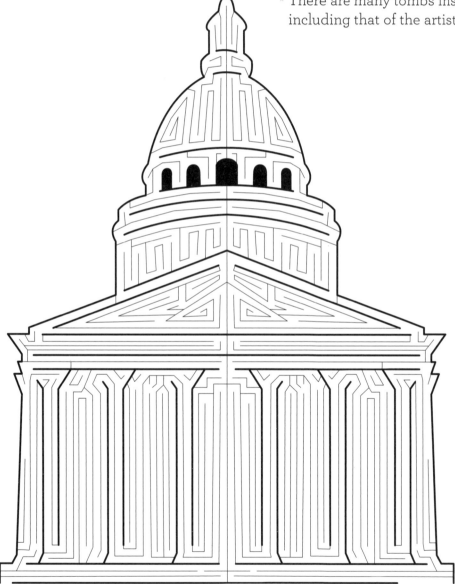

MOUNT KILIMANJARO

MODERATE

* Kilimanjaro isn't just Africa's highest mountain; it's the world's highest freestanding mountain and one of the biggest volcanoes on Earth.

* According to estimates, up to eight ice ages have allowed glaciers to remain on Kilimanjaro. The current ice is believed to have begun forming in 9700 BCE!

* Kilimanjaro is formed from two main volcanic peaks: Kibo and Mawenzi. Uhuru Peak on the Kibo summit is the highest point of the mountain—and Africa—at 19,341 feet.

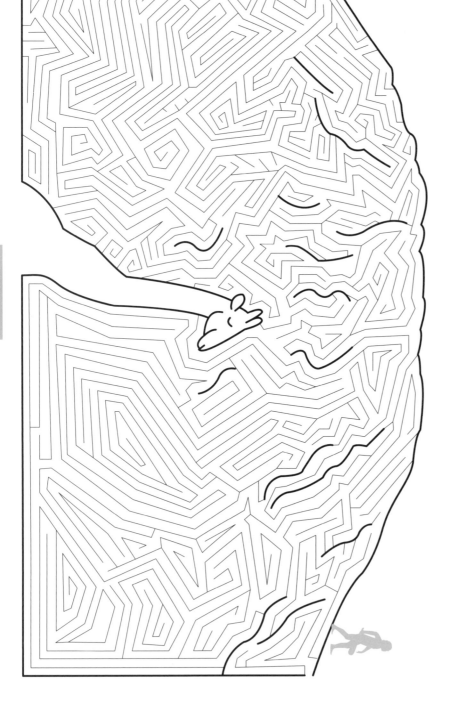

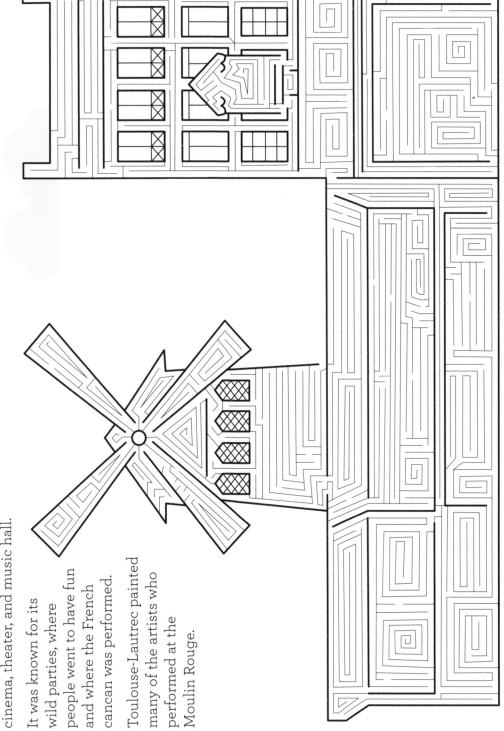

MOULIN ROUGE

* Founded in 1889, the Moulin Rouge (which means "red mill" in French) has been a cabaret, cinema, theater, and music hall.

* It was known for its wild parties, where people went to have fun and where the French cancan was performed.

* Toulouse-Lautrec painted many of the artists who performed at the Moulin Rouge.

DIFFICULT

CHÂTEAU FRONTENAC

* Château Frontenac is a grand hotel in the heart of Québec City.

* The original building was destroyed by fire in 1834, but it was rebuilt 60 years later.

* A 300-year-old stone bearing the Cross of Malta emblem can be seen in the hotel's lobby.

MODERATE

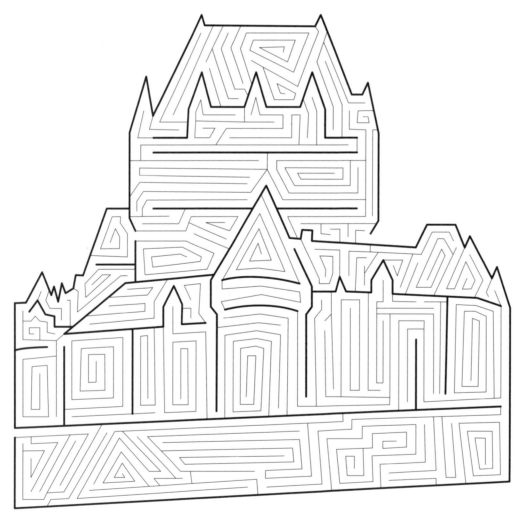

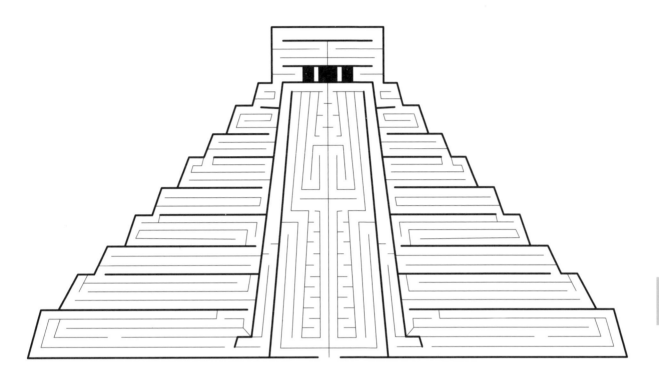

CHICHÉN ITZÁ

* Now ruins, Chichén Itzá was the largest city built by the Mayan people.

* A large stepped pyramid still survives. It was called El Castillo—"the castle"—by Spanish explorers, who thought it was a fortress.

* The pyramid actually represents the Mayan calendar. The 18 terraces on each side match the number of months in the Mayan year.

CHRYSLER BUILDING

* The Chrysler Building held the title of Tallest Building in the World for just one year. It was overtaken by the Empire State Building in 1931 but is still the tallest brick building in the world (albeit with a steel frame).

* References in the design to vehicle parts such as hubcaps and hood ornaments reflect the building's commission by the Chrysler Motor Corporation.

* Considered to be one of the best examples of Art Deco architecture, it is one of the most distinctive buildings in New York.

EASY

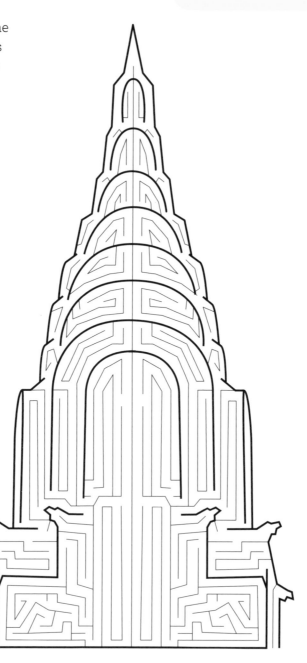

GLOBE OF SCIENCE AND INNOVATION

* The Globe of Science and Innovation, at the CERN center near Geneva, is a symbol of planet Earth.

* The huge dome is 89 feet high and 131 feet in diameter. It was constructed from 1,108 tons of wood.

* There is an exhibition space on the ground floor, and 300 neon tubes light up the globe at night.

GUGGENHEIM MUSEUM BILBAO

* The Guggenheim Museum Bilbao is an outstanding sculptural structure, designed by American architect Frank Gehry.

* The building, which was designed using cutting-edge design technology, is made of titanium, glass, and limestone.

* This expansive art gallery houses modern and contemporary artwork in 19 galleries, covering 118,403 square feet.

MODERATE

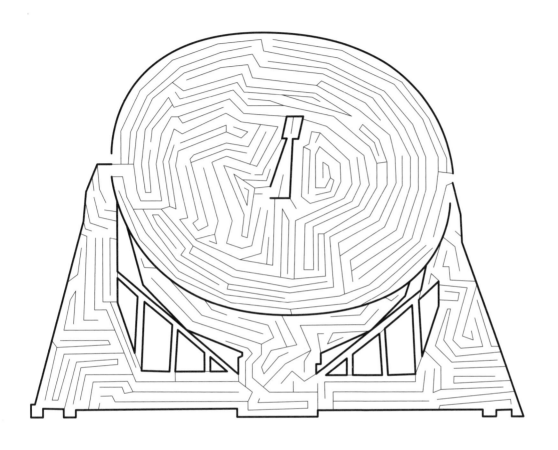

MODERATE

THE LOVELL TELESCOPE

* The Lovell Telescope, which weighs 3,527 tons, is a radio telescope.

* It has a huge white bowl, weighing 1,653 tons. The bowl is used to receive radio waves from space and focus them onto an antenna, which turns them into electrical signals.

* The electrical signals are sent to a computer, which turns them into a picture.

NYHAVN

* In the seventeenth century, Nyhavn was one of Copenhagen's busiest ports.

* The Danish fairy tale author Hans Christian Andersen wrote *The Princess and the Pea* when he lived in Nyhavn.

* Today, people go to Nyhavn to admire its colorful houses and to sit by the waterfront, have a meal, and listen to live music.

BRANDENBURG GATE

* The Brandenburg Gate in Berlin is made up of 12 columns and was commissioned by Friedrich Wilhelm II to symbolize peace.

* The famous chariot statue at the top of the gate was stolen by Napoleon in 1806. Eight years later, after his defeat, it was returned!

* Originally, only members of the royal family were allowed to walk through the central arch. Everyone else had to walk through the arches at either side.

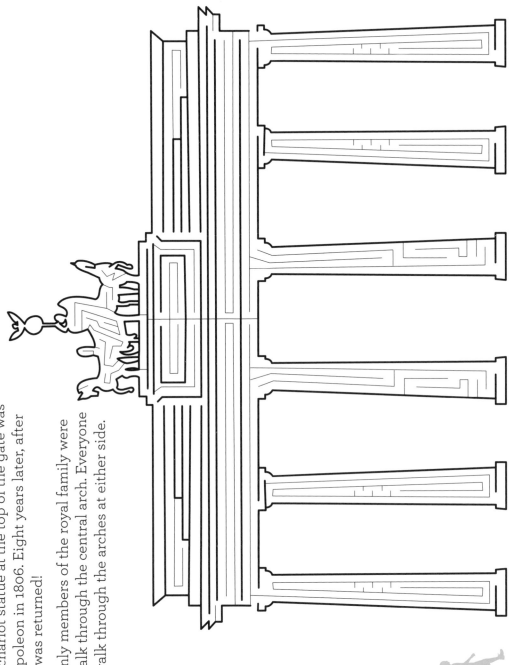

EASY

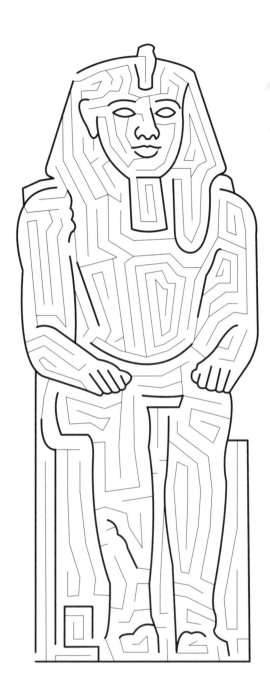

EASY

STATUE OF RAMSES II, LUXOR TEMPLE

* Luxor Temple is a huge complex that was built on the banks of the Nile River by the Ancient Egyptians. It once housed a village within its walls and is nicknamed "the world's largest outdoor museum."

* Ramses II built the First Pylon, one of several monumental gateways reaching 79 feet in height at the temple, decorated with scenes from his military triumphs.

* Ramses II was known for his extensive building programs during his long reign (from 1279–1213 BCE). Colossal statues of him, such as this one, can be found all over Egypt.

ST. JOSEPH'S ORATORY

* St. Joseph's Oratory is the largest church in Canada and is situated on the highest point in Montreal.

* The church has a large copper dome and was built in honor of St. Joseph, the patron saint of Canada.

* Two million visitors a year travel to see the church, with its spectacular stained-glass windows.

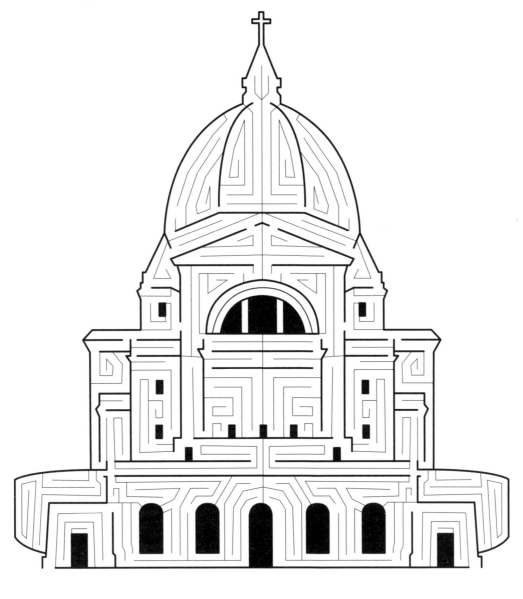

EASY

TAIPEI 101

* The design of the building is influenced by the shape of the native Chinese plant bamboo.

* Taipei 101 was the world's tallest building from 2004–2010, when it was surpassed in height by the Burj Khalifa in Dubai.

* Visitors to the tower's observation deck are whisked upward in elevators that travel from ground level to the 89th floor in 37 seconds!

BURJ KHALIFA

* As well as being the tallest building in the world, the Burj Khalifa also holds the record for the highest observation deck and the elevator with the longest travel distance in the world.

* The world's tallest free-standing structure, the Burj Khalifa has more than 160 stories and is over 2,717 feet in height.

* The tower was used as a filming location for the movie *Mission: Impossible—Ghost Protocol* (2011). It took 23 days to film a scene where Tom Cruise's character hangs from the outside of the building, with the actor insisting on carrying out the stunt himself!

EASY

THE WHITE HOUSE

* At various times in history, the White House has been known as the President's Palace, the President's House, and the Executive Mansion.

* It takes more than 660 gallons of paint in the shade Whisper White to cover the exterior of the White House.

* Electricity was first installed in 1891, during Benjamin Harrison's presidency. He was reportedly so nervous about its safety that he had a member of staff handle the light switches for him!

MODERATE

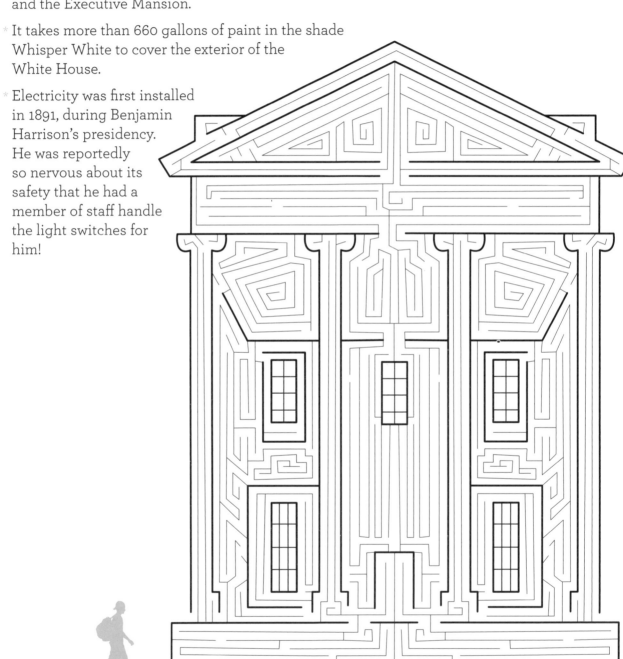

BUCKINGHAM PALACE

* Queen Victoria was the first monarch to live at Buckingham Palace after her coronation in 1837.

* The palace has 775 rooms, of which 78 are bathrooms. There's also a doctor's office, police station, and post office!

* Although Buckingham Palace survived nine direct hits from German bombs during the Blitz, King George VI and Queen Elizabeth remained in residence throughout World War II.

HOLLYWOOD SIGN

* Reading "HOLLYWOODLAND" until 1949, the famous Hollywood sign was constructed in 1923 to advertise a proposed housing development.

* When the sign needed renovating in 1973, Hugh Hefner held a fundraiser at the Playboy mansion to raise the $28,000 needed for each letter. Veteran rocker Alice Cooper owns an "O," and Hefner owned the "Y."

* To prevent people getting close to the sign, security measures now include razor wire, motion sensors, alarms, infrared technology, 24-hour monitoring, and helicopter patrols!

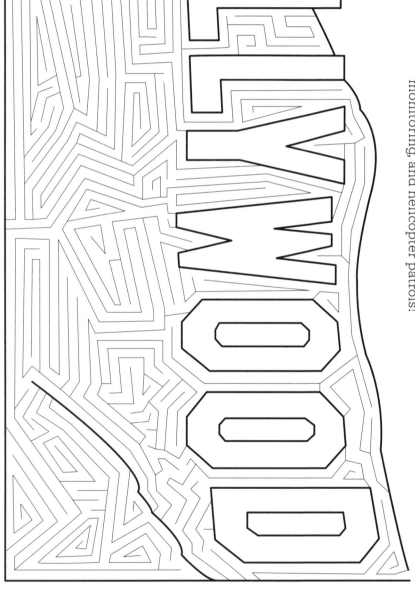

THE PARTHENON

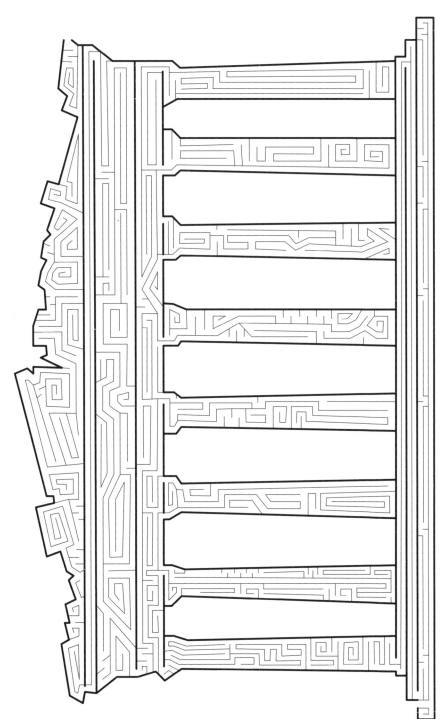

* The Parthenon temple was built between 447 and 432 BCE on the Athenian Acropolis.

* The building was dedicated to the patron deity of Athens, Athena, and it may have housed a wood, gold, and ivory statue of the goddess 39 feet tall.

* The temple was constructed of white marble and surrounded by 46 giant columns.

MODERATE

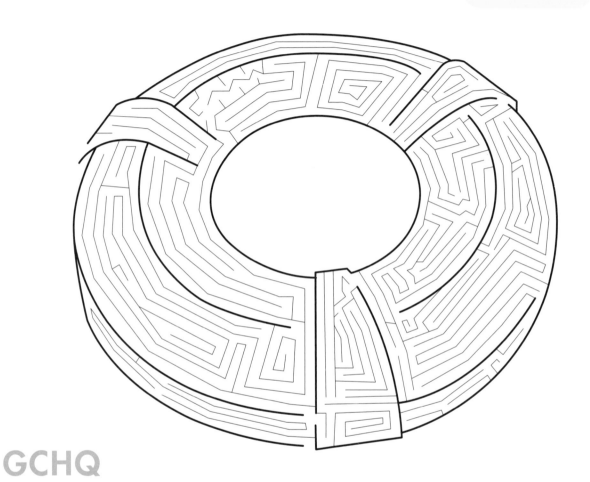

GCHQ

* GCHQ stands for Government Communications Headquarters, a British intelligence and security organization.

* At over 69 feet tall and with a diameter of over 591 feet, the GCHQ building cost $448,827,020 to construct.

* The building is known as "the Doughnut" because of its shape. At its center is a huge landscaped garden.

HEYDAR ALIYEV CENTER

* This dramatic, white, curved structure was built using glass-fiber-reinforced concrete panels.

* Situated in Azerbaijan's capital city, Baku, the center was named after the country's former president, Heydar Aliyev.

* Inside the building are a library, museum, conference center, and concert hall.

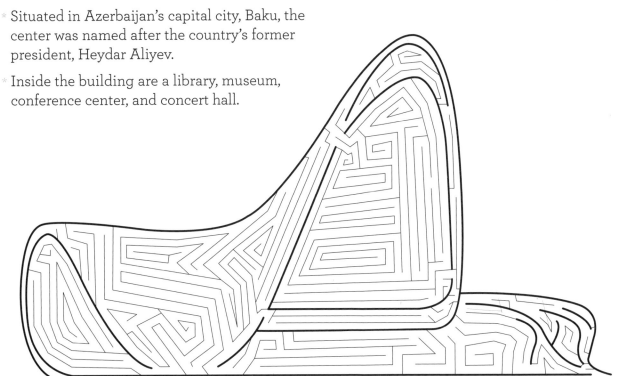

PORT ARTHUR

* Between 1830 and 1877 Port Arthur became a penal settlement. Thousands of convicts were transported there from the United Kingdom.

* Originally it was a timber site, and the convicts continued with this work, chopping trees to provide building material.

* Today, Port Arthur is a World Heritage Site and open-air museum.

POTALA PALACE

* Potala Palace is the highest ancient palace in the world, standing at 12,139 feet above sea level.

* The palace was built as the center of Tibetan government by the fifth Dalai Lama in 1645. It is thirteen stories high and has walls an average of 10 feet thick.

* Frescoes, murals, and artworks within the palace tell the history of the Tibetan people and the stories of different Dalai Lamas.

MODERATE

EDINBURGH CASTLE

* Castle Rock, upon which Edinburgh Castle is built, is part of an ancient extinct volcano.

* Legend has it that the ghost of a young bagpiper haunts the tunnels below the castle and that his music can still be heard there today....

* St. Margaret's Chapel in the grounds of the castle is the oldest surviving building in Scotland.

WESTMINSTER ABBEY

* The official name for Westminster Abbey is the Collegiate Church of St. Peter at Westminster.

* The current Westminster Abbey was built under the direction of King Henry III in the thirteenth century, with towers standing up to 225 feet tall.

* Charles Dickens, Sir Isaac Newton, and Charles Darwin are among the hundreds of famous people who are buried there.

DIFFICULT

77

GRIFFITH OBSERVATORY

* The founder of the observatory, Griffith J. Griffith, wanted to give the public an opportunity to use high-quality telescopes to view the stars.

* Since it opened in 1935, the Griffith Observatory's original telescope has been used by more than 7 million people.

* The facade of the building has been featured in over 300 films and television shows.

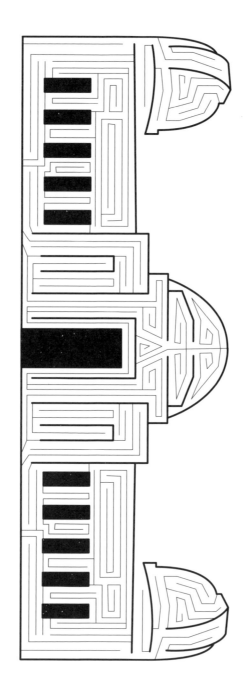

THE FORBIDDEN CITY

* The Forbidden City is the largest ancient palace in the world and receives over 14 million visitors every year.

* There are 9,999 rooms to explore within the site, contained inside 980 wooden buildings. The artifacts collected inside span thousands of years of Chinese history.

* An estimated 1 million laborers constructed the site, which is twice the size of the Vatican and three times the size of the Kremlin.

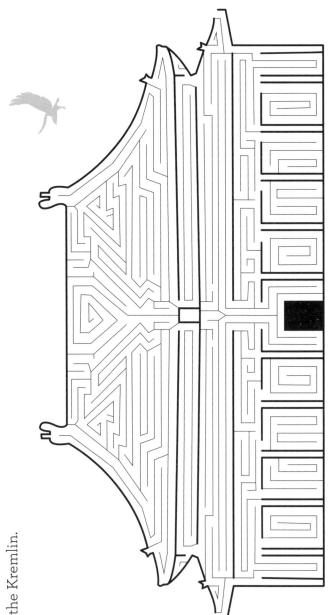

ALCATRAZ ISLAND

* Alcatraz Island is situated in the San Francisco Bay, off the coast of California.

* The most secure U.S. federal prison was built on Alcatraz Island and operated from 1934–1963. The prison was known as "the Rock."

* Some of the country's most notorious prisoners were held at the prison, including the gangster Al Capone.

BOROBUDUR

* This stone temple in central Java dates from the eighth and ninth centuries.

* The main temple is built in three levels around a hill. The base is shaped like a pyramid, with five square terraces. Above this is the trunk of a cone with three circular platforms.

* Around the platforms there are 72 bell-shaped monuments, each with a statue of Buddha.

MOUNT FUJI

* Mount Fuji is an active volcano located on Honshu Island in Japan. Its last eruption occurred in 1707.

* Also known as "Fuji-san," it is Japan's highest mountain at 12,388 feet tall.

* Mount Fuji is considered the sacred symbol of Japan and is surrounded by temples and shrines.

BEIJING NATIONAL STADIUM

* The stunning Beijing National Stadium was built to host the 2008 Olympic Games.

* It is the world's largest steel structure and is known as "the Bird's Nest" because of the shape of the roof, with its twisting steel sections.

* It cost $401,934,645 to build the stadium, which was carefully designed to withstand earthquakes.

EASY

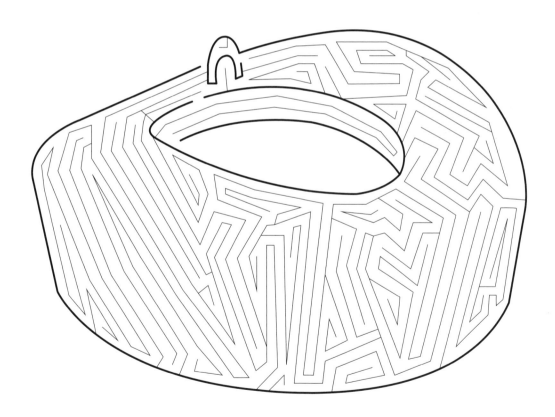

MODERATE

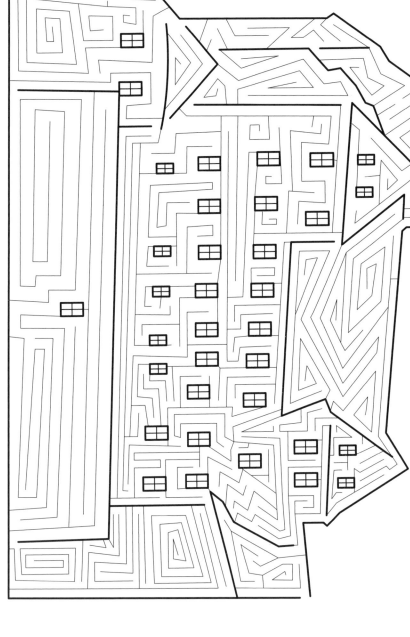

COLDITZ CASTLE

* Colditz Castle was built on a steep hill, 250 feet above the land around it. It is surrounded by stone walls 6.5 feet thick.

* The castle has been a hunting lodge and a hospital, but it's best known as a German prisoner-of-war camp for captured Allied officers during World War II.

* Despite the fortifications, many Allied prisoners managed to tunnel out of the castle, and 32 men escaped without being recaptured.

THE KELPIES

* At 98 feet tall, the Kelpies are the world's largest equine sculptures.

* 928 stainless-steel skin plates were used in total, with 1,323 tons of steel-reinforced concrete foundations per head. Each head weighs 331 tons.

* The sculpture was built on-site in just 90 days.

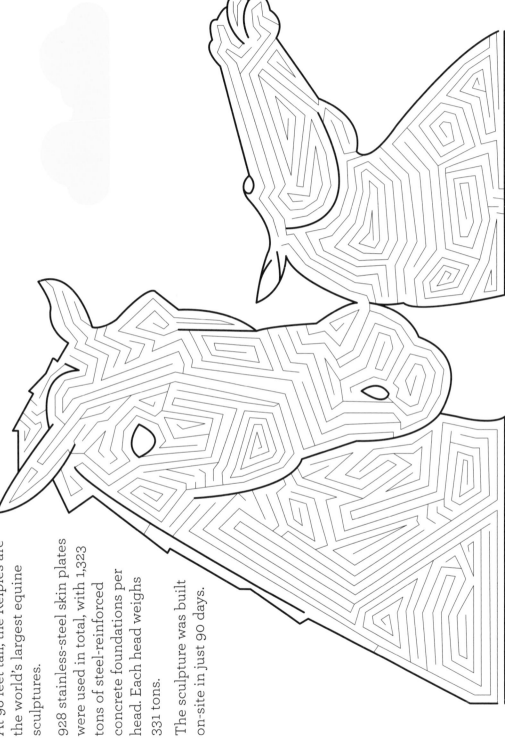

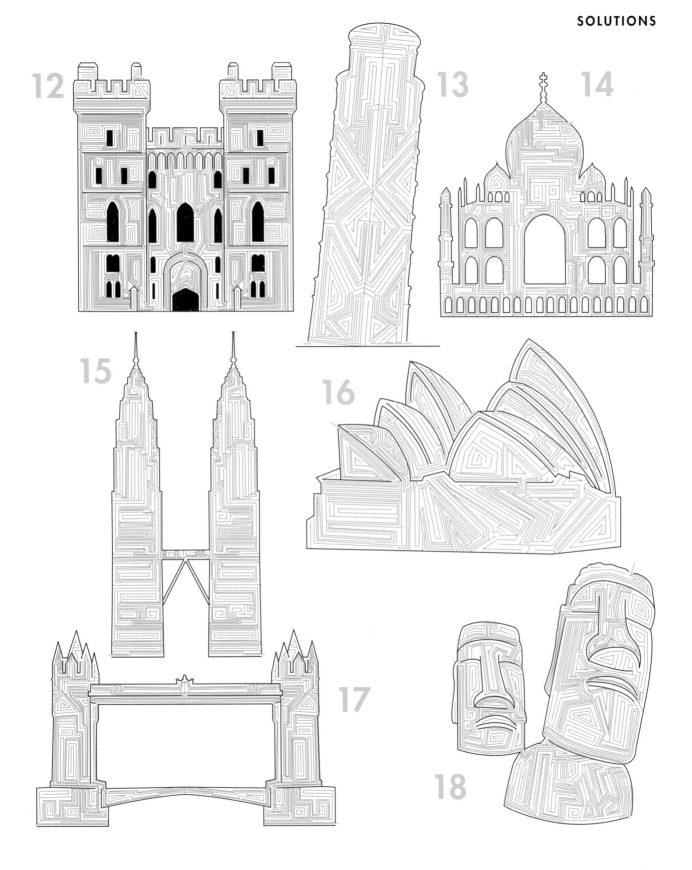

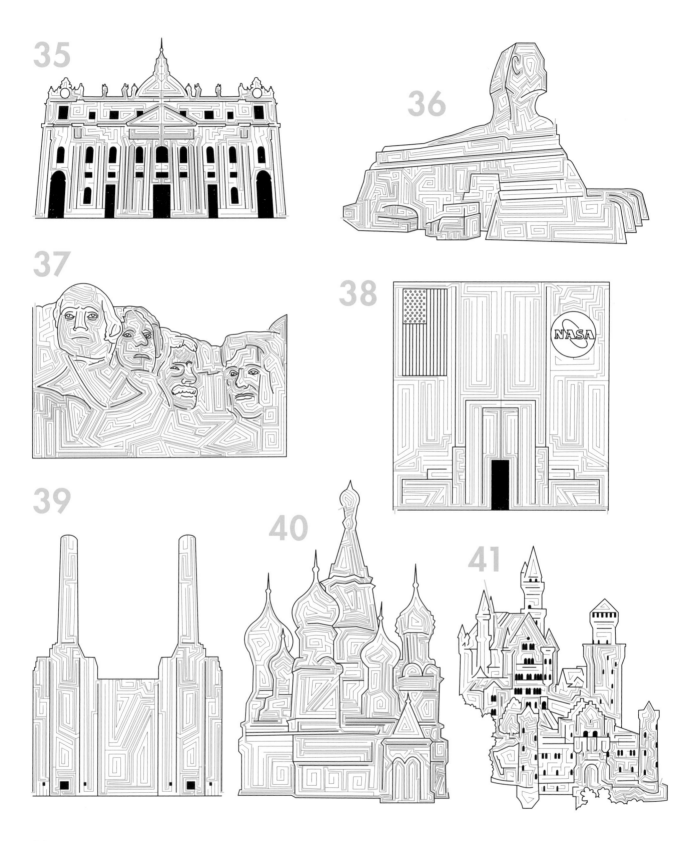

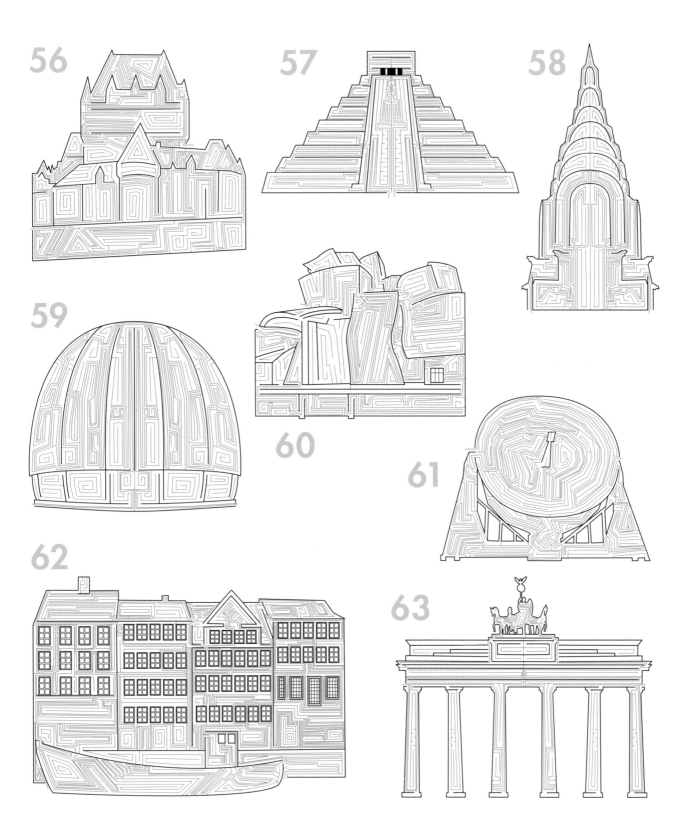

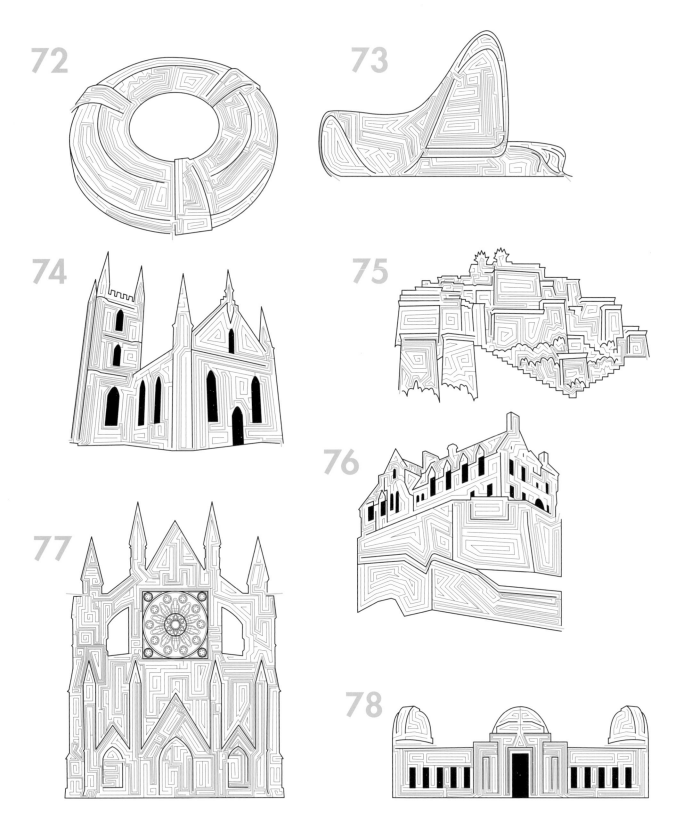

72

73

74

75

76

77

78